CONVERGE
Bible Studies

WHO IS JESUS?

Bible Studies

WHO IS JESUS?

ADAM THOMAS

Abingdon Press

Nashville

WHO IS JESUS?
CONVERGE BIBLE STUDIES

By Adam Thomas

Copyright © 2013 by Abingdon Press
All rights reserved.

Library of Congress Cataloging-in-Publication Data has been requested.

ISBN: 978-1-4267-7829-2

Series Editor: Shane Raynor

13 14 15 16 17 18 19 20 21 22—10 9 8 7 6 5 4 3 2 1

Manufactured in the United States of America

CONTENTS

ABOUT THE SERIES

Converge is a series of topical Bible studies based on the Common English Bible translation. Each title in the *Converge* series consists of four studies based around a common topic or theme. *Converge* brings together a unique group of writers from different backgrounds, traditions, and age groups.

HOW TO USE THESE STUDIES

Converge Bible studies can be used by small groups, classes, or individuals. Each study uses a simple format. For the convenience of the reader, the primary Scripture passages are included. In Insight and Ideas, the author of the study guide explores each Scripture passage, going deeper into the text and helping readers understand how the Scripture connects with the theme of the study. Questions are designed to encourage both personal reflection and group conversation. Some questions may not have simple answers. That's part of what makes studying the Bible so exciting.

Although Bible passages are included with each session, study participants may find it useful to have personal Bibles on hand for referencing other Scriptures. Converge studies are designed for use with the Common English Bible; but they work well with any modern, reliable translation.

ONLINE EXTRAS

Converge studies are available in both print and digital formats. Each title in the series has additional components that are available online, including companion articles, blog posts, extra questions, sermon ideas, and podcasts.

To access the companion materials, visit

http://www.MinistryMatters.com/Converge

Thanks for using Converge!

INTRODUCTION

Have you ever stopped to think just how much better Jesus Christ knows you than you know him? It's a pretty staggering thought, really. Not only that, but Jesus knows us better than we know ourselves. He's up 2–0. Now, while we will never be able to outscore Jesus in such a game, I believe that God delights in our following God's only Son; and part of that following is getting to know him just a little better than we already do—at least to score a few baskets in the game that Christ has in the bag.

Now, we don't want to fall into the trap of learning stuff "about" Jesus. That's like having someone tell you how awesome ice cream is without handing you a double-scoop cone. Rather, we want to know Jesus himself, as a friend or brother or guide (take your pick). This study invites you to get to know four elements of what makes Jesus who he is. And we'll discover that the more we know Jesus, the more Jesus will teach us who we are.

Thus, asking, "Who is Jesus?" (as the name of this study does) is not about facts and figures. We aren't going to study his height and weight and hair color, mostly since we don't know those things. Indeed, isn't it interesting that the Gospel writers never describe Jesus' physical appearance? We all have an image of Jesus in our minds (planted there by the cultural consciousness); but that image is little more than a flight of fancy, a pouring of Jesus into the mold of the majority ethnic group.

So if physical appearance is out, then how might we answer the question, "Who is Jesus?" We could start by telling a story about him, such as this one:

Jesus of Nazareth came from seemingly humble beginnings, although his mother knew better. At his birth, a disreputable cadre of outcasts claimed him as their savior; and that's what he was. His very name means "God saves." When he grew up, he left his mother's house, as sons often do; but that was perhaps the last normal thing he ever did.

"Change your hearts and your lives," he preached to any who would listen to his voice, saying that the kingdom of God is so close you can taste it. This was the good news his life pointed to, his Gospel. But that wasn't all. Every day, he revealed what it was like to live in God's kingdom, God's dream for all creation. He healed those who were sick and those who couldn't walk or see. He renewed the broken to wholeness; he gave hope to the despairing; and he welcomed everyone, especially those no one else would bother with, to his table. His words provoked peace, joy, and courage in some but, sadly, malice in others.

Jesus told his friends to love and serve others, come what may. He stood against the machinery of the world that enslaves people with false promises and misplaced priorities. He desired with every fiber of his being to replace the machine with a life lived fully in God, a life of blessing and abundance derived from God's promises, God's priorities. In the end, the machinery of the world felt threatened by this man, who was also so much more than a man—and for good reason. He was a threat. By putting Jesus to death— and a shameful death at that—the machine thought that it had won. But on the cross, Jesus gathered to himself all of the brokenness the world wrought, all that separates us from God—sin, shame, guilt, death—and their power died with him.

Three days after Jesus died, he rose again. Before dawn that Sunday morning, God the Father returned God the Son to us, resurrected as Jesus himself yet more than himself. He couldn't bear to break the promise to be with us always to the end of the ages, so he conquered death itself in order to stay in relationship with us into eternity. He breathed the peace of his Holy Spirit onto his friends, and we are still breathing those breaths even today.

We read this story in the accounts of Jesus' Gospel, but the story risks remaining simple words on the page if we don't also tell the story in our own lives. Our lives are extensions of the Gospel story because it never ended; it just moved from the lives of Jesus' followers to the page to our lives. As the final line of John's Gospel says, "Jesus did many other things as well. If all of them were recorded, I imagine the world itself wouldn't have enough room for the scrolls that would be written" (21:25).

We are those scrolls. We are extensions of Jesus' good news. Thus, asking, "Who is Jesus?" moves past the physical and the biographical and reaches for the relational. When we ask the question, what we really mean is, "How do you experience Jesus?" or "What is your relationship with Jesus?" or "How do you make Jesus known in your life?"

Think of it this way: If you were to ask me who Melinda is, I wouldn't first say that she's a writer/yoga instructor/life coach. I would say that she's my sister. I would start with this relationship first, before moving on to things "about" her. In the same vein, if you were to ask me, "Who is Jesus?" I would say that he is my guide, my teacher, my Lord. If I'm to be a participant in my relationship with Jesus, then (like in any good relationship) I should try to get to know him better.

Therefore, in this study, we focus on four elements of what makes Jesus who he is. First, we look at his names and examine how they are mission statements for his ministry. Second, we explore how we hear his voice, considering that we have no audio recordings of him. Third, we step into a showdown with Jesus and accept his life over our own false selves. And finally, we receive the four layers of peace that the Risen Christ gives to his disciples. In each of these sessions, we delve more deeply into who Jesus is. And in so doing, we discover how his identity makes us who we are.

1

THE NAMES OF JESUS
CHRIST'S PRESENCE AND SALVATION

SCRIPTURE
MATTHEW 1:18-25; ISAIAH 7:13-14; GENESIS 2:7

MATTHEW 1:18-25

[18]This is how the birth of Jesus Christ took place. When Mary his mother was engaged to Joseph, before they were married, she became pregnant by the Holy Spirit. [19]Joseph her husband was a righteous man. Because he didn't want to humiliate her, he decided to call off their engagement quietly. [20]As he was thinking about this, an angel from the Lord appeared to him in a dream and said, "Joseph son of David, don't be afraid to take Mary as your wife, because the child she carries was conceived by the Holy Spirit. [21]She will give birth to a son, and you will call him Jesus, because he will save his people from their sins." [22]Now all of this took place so that what the Lord had spoken through the prophet would be fulfilled:

*[23]Look! A virgin will become pregnant and give birth to a son,
And they will call him, Emmanuel.[a]*

(*Emmanuel* means "God with us.")

[24]When Joseph woke up, he did just as an angel from God commanded and took Mary as his wife. [25]But he didn't have sexual relations with her until she gave birth to a son. Joseph called him Jesus.

ISAIAH 7:13-14

[13]Then Isaiah said, "Listen, house of David! Isn't it enough for you to be tiresome for people that you are also tiresome before my God? [14]Therefore, the Lord will give you a sign. The young woman is pregnant and is about to give birth to a son, and she will name him Immanuel[b].

GENESIS 2:7

[7]The Lord God formed the human[c] from the topsoil of the fertile land[d] and blew life's breath into his nostrils. The human came to life.

---

a Isaiah 7:14
b Or *God is with us*
c Hebrew *adam*
d Hebrew *adamah*

INSIGHT AND IDEAS

By way of introduction in this first lesson, I'd like to tell you a little bit about my own birth narrative. No, it's not peculiar or noteworthy in any way; but it's mine, and I'd like to share it with you.

When my mother discovered that she was going to have a second child, she began thinking up names for the tiny person growing within her. Since she didn't know until I was born whether I was a boy or a girl, she tried all manner of names on for size. She spoke them loudly and softly, lovingly and reprovingly. She paired them with my sister Melinda's name. She let them roll off her tongue, and she wrote them down to see how they looked on paper. Finally, she settled on a boy's name—a real winner. Lying in bed one morning, she struck up a conversation with my father: "I think we should name him Tristram."

My father sat bolt upright in bed. "Absolutely not," he said. And so with a mixture of brainstorming, cajoling, and bargaining, my parents settled on Adam, thinking the name to be a good, strong one.

Sometimes, I wonder what my life would be like had my dad agreed with my mother's initial offering. Tristram is certainly less common than Adam—not that Adam is on a top ten baby name list. Tristram comes from the word *sad* in Latin or *tumult* in Gaelic. The variant Tristan was one of King Arthur's knights, the subject of stories and songs, and a title character in Wagner's great opera *Tristan and Isolde*. You know where Adam comes from. When God sculpted the dust into a form and breathed life into the body, what God made was my name. The second creation story in the Book of Genesis tells the story like this:

> On the day the Lord God made earth and sky—before any wild plants appeared on the earth, and before any field crops grew, because the Lord God hadn't yet sent rain on the earth and there was still no human being to farm the fertile land, though a stream rose from the earth and watered all of the fertile land—the Lord God formed the human from the topsoil of the fertile land and blew life's breath into his nostrils. The human came to life. (Genesis 2:5-7)

Notice that Adam isn't in there—well, not as a name at least. Originally, my name wasn't a name at all. Rather, *Adam— ha adam,* in Hebrew—was the word for "human being." "Person of earth" might be the most expressive translation.

DO NAMES MATTER?

Would my life be any different had I been named Tristram rather than Adam? Could I have traced a different path with a different name? Does a name really matter in the grand scheme of things? Judging by the opening chapter of the Gospel according to Matthew, the answer is yes. The Gospel starts with a long list of names, all of the generations from Abraham up to Joseph, husband of Mary. Three sets of fourteen generations: forty-seven names in all, since Matthew mentions the names of a few special women. Then in the very next passage, an angel from the Lord comes to Joseph in a dream and directs Joseph's naming procedure.

In Matthew 1:18-25, we see that the right name is significant enough for an angel to tell Joseph just what to call the child growing in his fiancée's womb. But just one name won't do: Matthew recalls a second name for this child, from the words of the great prophet Isaiah. And these names—Jesus and Emmanuel—these names are more than just names. They are mission statements. They are explanations of the life that God sent God's only Son to live.

The angel in Joseph's dream tells him to name Mary's child Jesus, because "he will save his people from their sins" (verse 21). *Jesus* (*Iesous*) is the Greek way of writing the Hebrew name *Yeshua,* which we render in English as *Joshua*. In the Hebrew Scriptures, Moses grooms Joshua to be his successor because Moses knows that he's not going to reach the Promised Land. Moses makes sure that all of the Israelites know that Joshua is his choice.

> Then Moses called Joshua and, with all Israel watching, said to him: "Be strong and fearless because you are the one who will lead this people to the land the Lord swore to their ancestors to give to them; you are the one who will divide up the land for them. But the Lord is the one who is marching before you! He is the one who will be with you! He won't let you down. He won't abandon you. So don't be afraid or scared!" (Deuteronomy 31:7-8)

After Moses dies, Joshua leads the people of Israel out of the wilderness, which had encompassed them for forty years. This hero of the old stories, which were told at the Temple and in the synagogue and around the dinner table for hundreds of years, finishes the work of bringing the people into the Promised Land. Forty years from God's initial rescue of God's people from slavery in Egypt, Joshua helps God close that chapter of Israel's history.

GOD SAVES

God saves Israel. This is the mission statement found in Joshua's name, which means "God saves." The life that Mary's child will live years after Joseph gives the boy Joshua's name accomplishes the same mission. Jesus, the angel says, "will save his people from their sins" (Matthew 1:21). Jesus takes the people out of the new wilderness in which they are wandering. This new wilderness takes up no space on a map. There is no Promised Land a month's hard trudging through the desert. Rather, the wilderness from which Jesus saves the people is the emotional, psychological, and spiritual desolation that they wrought for themselves. They created deserts around and within themselves through misplaced priorities and apathy toward the less fortunate and worship of all manner of idols, including the very Law that was supposed to connect them to God.

Sound familiar? The desolation that the people of Jesus' time brought upon themselves is the same desolation that affects people today. Our idols might be shiny and new, but our deference to them is unchanged. Notice, however, that the mission statement found in Jesus' Hebrew name is not

"God saved," but "God saves." With his resurrection, Jesus signals to people of all times that nothing in all creation—not even death—can keep God from bringing people back to God. We are some of those people.

Nothing in all creation can keep Jesus from being in relationship with us. Recall Paul's triumphant words to the church in Rome:

> "I'm convinced that nothing can separate us from God's love in Christ Jesus our Lord: not death or life, not angels or rulers, not present things or future things, not powers or height or depth, or any other thing that is created." (Romans 8:38-39)

When we embrace this joyous truth, we can participate with the saving acts of God, which Jesus' name makes known. We can participate with Jesus in turning our desolate deserts into Promised Lands.

GOD WITH US

This constant relationship, this promise kept through the power of the resurrection, brings us to the mission statement found in Jesus' other name: Emmanuel. For this name, the angel in Matthew's Gospel reaches back to the words of the prophet Isaiah:

> Then Isaiah said, "Listen, house of David! Isn't it enough for you to be tiresome for people that you are also tiresome before my God? Therefore, the Lord will give you a sign. The young woman is pregnant and is about to give birth to a son, and she will name him Immanuel." (Isaiah 7:13-14)

Matthew helps out his non-Hebrew readers by translating this name right there in the text. *Emmanuel* means "God with us." Just as God was with Moses and Joshua and the rest of Israel during their forty-year journey through the wilderness, God was still with the people of Israel during their own self-imposed desolation. After all, God is the God of the desert and the Promised Land. But their desolation kept them from seeing the truth that God was with them. In Jesus' life, the reality of Emmanuel—God with us—found flesh and blood.

After centuries of captivity and occupation, after the life-giving words of the prophets had begun to fade from the collective memory, God's people needed the immediacy, the physicality of the Incarnation—of the embodiment of God-with-us—to bring them back to God. This flesh and blood reality of Emmanuel shocked some folks out of their desolation. They told others and those others told more, and pretty soon, followers of Jesus Christ were spreading to the ends of the earth his good news of abundant life lived for God.

But just as "God saves" is not simply a past event, "God-with-us" emanates from Jesus' life on earth through the presence of the Holy Spirit down to us. At the end of the Gospel according to Matthew, Jesus echoes his second name when he says to the disciples: "Look, I myself will be with you every day until the end of this present age" (Matthew 28:20b). Here Jesus promises to continue to fulfill his name's mission statement. That present age is still present. We, too, can encounter Emmanuel in our lives.

Every moment of every day, we have the opportunity of encountering the presence of God-with-us. We have the ability to participate with the God who saves in turning our desolation into a place of springs, where the "desert and the dry land will be glad" and "the wilderness will rejoice and blossom" (Isaiah 35:1). In the very names of our Savior Jesus Christ, we find the good news of God for all people. When we discover the presence of Emmanuel and embrace the forgiveness and salvation of Yeshua, of Jesus, we can then begin to ask God what our missions shall be. We can pray, "O God, what would you have our names mean?"

QUESTIONS

1. What does Scripture mean by *righteous* (Matthew 1:19)? What was Joseph's original plan when he discovered that Mary was pregnant?

2. Imagine the conversation when Mary first told Joseph about her pregnancy. How might have sounded? Why, do you think, did God wait to speak to Joseph in a dream (Matthew 1:20)?

3. The angel instructed Joseph to name the baby Jesus. What was the significance of names in the first century? How important are names now?

4. In connection with Christ's mission, how does the name *Emmanuel* complement the name *Jesus*?

5. *Joshua* is the English rendering of the name *Jesus*. How does Jesus' ministry and mission compare with Joshua's in the Old Testament?

6. Why is the fact that Jesus is "God-with-us" so extraordinary?

7. How is Jesus' dual mission (God saves and God with us) still relevant in the twenty-first century? How do we communicate this effectively to a modern audience?

8. First Corinthians 15:45 calls Jesus "the last Adam." What does this mean?

9. What does your name mean? (You can find out using a baby name book or by searching online for name meanings.) Do you believe that your name has played a role in who you are today?

10. Out of what desert or wilderness are you journeying through that you need Jesus to lead you?

2

THE VOICE OF JESUS
LISTENING TO THE SHEPHERD

SCRIPTURE
JOHN 10:1-30

¹I assure you that whoever doesn't enter into the sheep pen through the gate but climbs over the wall is a thief and an outlaw. ²The one who enters through the gate is the shepherd of the sheep. ³The guard at the gate opens the gate for him, and the sheep listen to his voice. He calls his own sheep by name and leads them out. ⁴Whenever he has gathered all of his sheep, he goes before them and they follow him, because they know his voice. ⁵They won't follow a stranger but will run away because they don't know the stranger's voice." ⁶Those who heard Jesus use this analogy didn't understand what he was saying.

⁷So Jesus spoke again, "I assure you that I am the gate of the sheep. ⁸All who came before me were thieves and outlaws, but the sheep didn't listen to them. ⁹I am the gate. Whoever enters through me will

be saved. They will come in and go out and find pasture. [10]The thief enters only to steal, kill, and destroy. I came so that they could have life—indeed, so that they could live life to the fullest.

[11]"I am the good shepherd. The good shepherd lays down his life for the sheep. [12]When the hired hand sees the wolf coming, he leaves the sheep and runs away. That's because he isn't the shepherd; the sheep aren't really his. So the wolf attacks the sheep and scatters them. [13]He's only a hired hand and the sheep don't matter to him.

[14]"I am the good shepherd. I know my own sheep and they know me, [15]just as the Father knows me and I know the Father. I give up my life for the sheep. [16]I have other sheep that don't belong to this sheep pen. I must lead them too. They will listen to my voice and there will be one flock, with one shepherd.

[17]"This is why the Father loves me: I give up my life so that I can take it up again. [18]No one takes it from me, but I give it up because I want to. I have the right to give it up, and I have the right to take it up again. I received this commandment from my Father."

[19]There was another division among the Jews because of Jesus' words. [20]Many of them said, "He has a demon and has lost his mind. Why listen to him?" [21]Others said, "These aren't the words of someone who has a demon. Can a demon heal the eyes of people who are blind?"

[22]The time came for the Festival of Dedication in Jerusalem. It was winter, [23]and Jesus was in the temple, walking in the covered

porch named for Solomon. [24]The Jewish opposition circled around him and asked, "How long will you test our patience? If you are the Christ, tell us plainly."

[25]Jesus answered, "I have told you, but you don't believe. The works I do in my Father's name testify about me, [26]but you don't believe because you don't belong to my sheep. [27]My sheep listen to my voice. I know them and they follow me. [28]I give them eternal life. They will never die, and no one will snatch them from my hand. [29]My Father, who has given them to me, is greater than all, and no one is able to snatch them from my Father's hand. [30]I and the Father are one."

INSIGHT AND IDEAS

I'm sure that we can all agree that making a real audible connection with Jesus is difficult. After all, our Lord ascended into heaven two thousand years ago, give or take a few years. You can't download his parables from iTunes. You can't watch the Sermon on the Mount on YouTube. You can't get a podcast of the Last Supper. As Judas sings at the end of *Jesus Christ Superstar*: "If you'd come today, you could have reached the whole nation. Israel in 4 B.C. had no mass communication."

With no way to make that real audible connection with Jesus, we might be tempted to disregard the first sixteen verses of John 10 as an antiquated relic of Jesus' own time.

In this section, John records Jesus discussing his identity as the good shepherd who takes care of the sheep. This is as close to a standard parable as John gets; rather, for John, Jesus *is* the parable. So it makes sense when a few verses later, John makes sure we know that Jesus is talking about himself when discussing the art of shepherding. Here Jesus is speaking with some of his opponents, who get ready to stone him for these words:

> "My sheep listen to my voice. I know them and they follow me. I give
> them eternal life. They will never die, and no one will snatch them
> from my hand. My Father, who has given them to me, is greater than
> all, and no one is able to snatch them from my Father's hand. I and
> the Father are one." (John 10:27-30)

"My sheep listen to my voice," says Jesus. The fact that you are engaging in this Bible study tells me that on some level you identify as a member of Jesus' flock. So with no person to speak or recording to play, how do we, his sheep, hear Jesus' voice? How do we listen to someone who lived twenty centuries ago and who inhabited the other side of the world and who spoke a language that no longer exists?

HOW WE HEAR JESUS' VOICE

All those barriers notwithstanding, we sheep still hear Jesus' voice. We hear his voice in myriad ways, too many to list exhaustively during this reflection. So here are three: We hear Jesus speak to us from within ourselves, from the collective voice of the community, and from the prayerful reading of his words in the Gospel.

THROUGH SCRIPTURE

Let's begin with the reading of Scripture. Did you know that in the ancient world in which the Bible was written, silent reading was very uncommon? People read aloud even when they were alone. The Book of Acts presents a clear example of this. Philip is walking along the road from Jerusalem to Gaza when he happens upon an Ethiopian eunuch reading the prophet Isaiah. How does Philip know that the eunuch is reading Isaiah? Right—because the eunuch is reading out loud to himself.

> [The Ethiopian eunuch] was reading the prophet Isaiah while sitting in his carriage. The Spirit told Philip, "Approach this carriage and stay with it." Running up to the carriage, Philip heard the man reading the prophet Isaiah. He asked, "Do you really understand what you are reading?" The man replied, "Without someone to guide me, how could I?" Then he invited Philip to climb up and sit with him. (Acts 8:28-31)

Now, we all grew up with elementary school teachers giving us cross looks if we accidentally began reading aloud when we were supposed to be reading silently. I also imagine that were I to begin reading a novel out loud on the subway, I might engender some strong negative reactions.

Obviously, our culture no longer subscribes to the ancient practice of reading everything out loud. But in our efforts to be the sheep who hear Jesus' voice, I invite you to attempt this practice. Read the Gospel slowly, prayerfully, carefully, and *audibly*. Listen to the sound of your own voice speaking the words of Jesus:

"Come to me, all you who are struggling hard and carrying heavy loads, and I will give you rest." (Matthew 11:28)

"I assure you that when you have done it for one of the least of these brothers and sisters of mine, you have done it for me." (Matthew 25:40)

"I myself will be with you every day until the end of this present age." (Matthew 28:20)

Hear the voice of Jesus welling up from within you. Feel your mouth and tongue and breath work in concert to form those life-giving words. When you encounter a particular verse or passage that strikes you, don't rush through the words. Sit with them. Say them aloud and hear Jesus speaking through you, to you. Make those words your breath prayer. Practice making the voice of Jesus the first thing that comes to your own lips in idle moments and joyful moments and fearful moments alike. As Paul says to the church in Colossae, "The word of Christ must live in you richly" (Colossians 3:16). We sheep hear Jesus' voice in the words of Scripture when we attend to them and attune to them and orient our lives around them.

WITHIN OURSELVES

This orientation continues in our own interior lives, which is the next setting for hearing the voice of Jesus. At the outset of his own trek through the inward life, St. Augustine says, "My God, I would have no being, I would not have any existence, unless you were in me. Or rather, I would have no being if I were not in you." Because we are in God and God somehow dwells within us, we can access the voice of Jesus within ourselves.

Most often, we are too distracted by external stimuli to attend to this voice. And when we manage to find grace enough to silence the outward bombardment, we still must contend with the chattering voice of our own selfish desire. This seductive voice constantly eats away at us, eroding us with whatever idols happen to be fashionable this season. But underneath the artillery and the idolatry, another voice speaks. This is the voice of Jesus speaking softly enough that we have to strain to hear. And everyone knows that when you have to strain to hear, you must be listening.

This internal voice of Jesus is the same still small voice that Elijah hears on the mountain after the wind and the earthquake and the fire pass by (1 Kings 19:12). This is the same voice that the psalmist hears when God says, "Be still, and know that I am God" (Psalm 46:10). The voice of Jesus speaks truth into our souls every moment of every day; and every once in a great while, we might happen to stop and hear that truth.

I remember a time in my life in which each day, I asked God whether I was in the right relationship. And each day, I felt the resonance in my chest of a deep and abiding, "Yes." Then on a day of no particular consequence, the resonance disappeared. But rather than paying attention to the change, I forced myself to remember what the voice sounded like. And for months, I lied to myself rather than making the effort to listen to Christ's voice within me. When the relationship ended, I was shocked; although I had no right to be. The voice of Jesus had been preparing me for that outcome. The still small voice speaks to us continually. All we need do is listen.

FROM THE COMMUNITY

We sheep hear Jesus' voice in our inner selves, but without that voice also speaking to us from a loving community, the dialogue is incomplete. "The word of Christ must live in you richly," says Paul, and he continues, "Teach and warn each other with all wisdom by singing psalms, hymns, and spiritual songs. Sing to God with gratitude in your hearts" (Colossians 3:16). Without this conversation, this communion with one another, we struggle to discern the voice of Jesus in our lives. God calls each one of us to ministry both within the church and in our lives outside the walls of the church. The voice of the community and the internal voice within each of us coalesce to form our calls to serve God.

In the Episcopal tradition to which I belong, we often renew our baptismal promises. One promise asks, "Will you seek and serve Christ in all persons, loving your neighbor as yourself?" When we answer, "I will, with God's help," we signal our willingness to listen to the voice of Jesus speaking through one another. If we are able to sublimate the chattering voices of our own selfish desire, then each still small voice within us can join with the next, creating the voice of Jesus in the community. When we share in one another's lives, when we take the time to know one another on deep, personal levels, we more readily serve as vessels for the voice of Jesus to one another.

'MY SHEEP LISTEN TO MY VOICE'

Christ's voice in the Gospel forms and guides the other two voices—the interior voice and the voice of the community. Working together, this threefold voice of Jesus speaks to us across the barriers of time and distance and language. Jesus proclaims, "My sheep listen to my voice." This statement is both a declaration and a hope. As we struggle with our flurries of distractions and entanglements both externally and internally, I pray that we each find the grace to take seriously these words of Jesus: "My sheep listen to my voice" (John 10:27). We are his sheep. I hear Jesus' voice calling each of us to serve one another in love and reach out with healing arms to a broken world. What do you hear?

QUESTIONS

1. Who is the thief and the outlaw in John 10:1? Who are the sheep (John 10:2)?

2. Who is the shepherd of the sheep (John 10:2)? What is the significance of the gate?

3. How do the sheep know the shepherd's voice (John 10:4)? Why was this analogy apparently so hard for its initial hearers to understand (John 10:6)?

4. Who might the hired hand represent in John 10:12? Who is the wolf (John 10:11)?

5. Why does Jesus compare his relationship to the sheep with his relationship to God (John 10:15)?

6. Who are the "other sheep" Jesus speaks of (John 10:16)?

7. What is remarkable about John 10:18? How might this challenge some perceptions of the life and death of Jesus?

8. Why were the Jews so divided over Jesus' words (John 10:19)? Why doesn't Jesus explicitly claim to be the Christ in this passage (John 10:24)?

9. What is the eternal life Jesus gives to his sheep (John 10:28)? What does Jesus mean when he says that he and "the Father are one" (John 10:30)?

10. How does God speak to people through Scripture? Describe a time when God has spoken through a passage of Scripture to a situation you were facing.

11. How do we learn to hear Christ's voice within ourselves? How do we know that it's not some other voice or our imagination?

12. Why is it important to listen for Christ's voice in community with one another?

13. What do we do when voices we think are Christ's appear to contradict each other?

14. What are some steps you can take to hear the voice of Jesus more clearly?

3

THE LIFE OF JESUS
SURRENDERING OUR LIVES TO CHRIST

SCRIPTURE
MARK 8:34-38; GALATIANS 2:16-21; PHILIPPIANS 3:8-11

MARK 8:34-38

[34]After calling the crowd together with his disciples, Jesus said to them, "All who want to come after me must say no to themselves, take up their cross, and follow me. [35]All who want to save their lives will lose them. But all who lose their lives because of me and because of the good news will save them. [36]Why would people gain the whole world but lose their lives? [37]What will people give in exchange for their lives? [38]Whoever is ashamed of me and my words in this unfaithful and sinful generation, the Human One[a] will be ashamed of that person when he comes in the Father's glory with the holy angels.

---

a Or Son of Man

GALATIANS 2:16-21

[16]However, we know that a person isn't made righteous by the works of the Law but rather through the faithfulness of Jesus Christ. We ourselves believed in Christ Jesus so that we could be made righteous by the faithfulness of Christ and not by the works of the Law—because no one will be made righteous by the works of the Law. [17]But if it is discovered that we ourselves are sinners while we are trying to be made righteous in Christ, then is Christ a servant of sin? Absolutely not! [18]If I rebuild the very things that I tore down, I show that I myself am breaking the Law. [19]I died to the Law through the Law, so that I could live for God. [20]I have been crucified with Christ and I no longer live, but Christ lives in me. And the life that I now live in my body, I live by faith, indeed, by the faithfulness of God's Son, who loved me and gave himself for me. [21]I don't ignore the grace of God, because if we become righteous through the Law, then Christ died for no purpose.

PHILIPPIANS 3:8-11

[8]But even beyond that, I consider everything a loss in comparison with the superior value of knowing Christ Jesus my Lord. I have lost everything for him, but what I lost I think of as sewer trash, so that I might gain Christ [9]and be found in him. In Christ I have a righteousness that is not my own and that does not come from the Law but rather from the faithfulness of Christ. It is the righteousness of God that is based on faith. [10]The righteousness that I have comes from knowing Christ, the power of his

resurrection, and the participation in his sufferings. It includes being conformed to his death [11]so that I may perhaps reach the goal of the resurrection of the dead.

INSIGHT AND IDEAS

I'm sure that we've all watched this scene unfold in a film, a Western, perhaps starring John Wayne or Gary Cooper. The sheriff checks the rounds in his six-shooter; puts on his Stetson and shiny, star-shaped badge; and walks bowlegged out of his tin-roofed station. His spurs clink as he walks, and his shoes kick up the dust of the main street running through town. At the same time, the bat-wing doors of the saloon swing outward, and the gun-slinging outlaw swaggers down the steps into the street. The outlaw wears a black bandana and black chaps and keeps his Colt .45 slung low on his hip, the better to draw quickly. They face each other at high noon out on the street. They are alone, although the whole town is watching from windows and rooftops. A tumbleweed skitters across the road between them. There are no shadows. And the sheriff says, "This town ain't big enough for the both of us."

With these words, the sheriff gives the outlaw the chance to turn himself in or to leave town before the inevitable shoot-out. But the shoot-out is inevitable for two reasons: First, the movie-going public would be disappointed in a Western without a shoot-out; and second, the outlaw's very nature and personality won't let him go quietly.

JESUS GIVES US A CHOICE

If Mark 8:34-38 were staged as a Western, you and I would be cast as the outlaw. And a Stetson-wearing Jesus would be the sheriff, who says to us, "This town ain't big enough for the both of us."

But in the Western rendition of this scene, Jesus wouldn't be talking about a town. He would be talking about us, about our souls, about our lives. "This *life* ain't big enough for the both of us" is the Western film translation of Jesus' words: "All who want to come after me must say no to themselves, take up their cross, and follow me. All who want to save their lives will lose them. But all who lose their lives because of me and because of the good news will save them."

With these words, Jesus gives us the same choice the sheriff gives the outlaw. We can surrender ourselves to Christ, or we can fight in an attempt to keep control of our lives. We cannot, however, do both.

At first glance, the second option seems quite appealing. Who wouldn't want to remain in control of his or her own life? Is that not the American dream—self-determination, self-preservation, pulling oneself up by one's own bootstraps? Do we Americans not prize the entrepreneur, the independent thinker, the individual who defies the odds to become someone? Of course, we do. In and of themselves, these things are not bad. But they can lead us down some wrong paths.

Let's take self-preservation, for example. As infants, this is the only thought in our little brains. We cry whenever we perceive that something is being withheld that will help us thrive. We are incapable of taking care of ourselves on our own; so we induce, through love and tears, others to take care of us. At this stage of our life, self-preservation is not a choice. Keeping ourselves going is a hardwired imperative of our biology. As we grow up and become more self-sustaining, the affinity for self-preservation that we displayed as infants stays with us. The biological imperative keeps us seeking things that will help us survive.

Again, this is not a bad thing at all. The problems begin when the "self" we are trying to preserve starts wandering away from those life-giving things that helped us thrive as infants. Some of those life-giving things—such as family and love—can remain throughout our lives; but other, life-taking things can crowd them out. In middle school, we define ourselves based on the insecure input of our peers and the warped input of the consumer culture. Remember that? What horrible years, for the popular and the unpopular alike. In young adult life, we define ourselves based on our (never quite good enough) physical attractiveness to prospective mates. Remember that? Have you ever looked in the mirror and truly been satisfied with what you saw there? In adult life, we define ourselves based on our work and our need to be comfortable.

GOING IN THE WRONG DIRECTION

When these definitions lead us down life-taking paths, we humans have a tendency to follow such paths to the extreme. We become addicted to alcohol or drugs or gambling or videogames. We pursue what marketing experts define as success. We take on the lone wolf persona, ignoring the welfare of others because we perceive that we are not faring well enough ourselves. Pretty soon, the selves that we have become look so very little like the selves God created us to be.

What life-taking paths have you wandered down? What seduced you with a quick fix but led ultimately to an erosion of the self? Perhaps it was a need or a craving that steered you in the wrong direction, like the grocery cart with the bad wheel. Perhaps it was a relationship that you knew deep down was no good for you but which you continued with anyway because you convinced yourself that it was better than nothing. Perhaps it was something that originally had laudable goals but that degenerated into grubbing self-interest masked in a veneer of respectability. Whatever our life-taking paths are, they turn us into unrecognizable versions of ourselves—at least as compared to the vision of us that God yearns to see.

The tricky thing is this: The farther down the life-taking paths we go, the deeper the need to preserve these false selves becomes. We know no other way to live. We have no idea what another path would like; and the life-taking ones tend to be dark and overgrown with brambles, which shut out all of the other paths we could be taking. Not to mention that if we tried another path, we'd be moving into uncharted territory; and the unknown is the scariest reality of all. So we cling hard. We preserve these so-called lives.

And we become outlaws in our own bodies, betrayers of the abundant life that God desires for each of us.

To these outlaws, Jesus says, "This life ain't big enough for the both of us." But instead of drawing his six-shooter, like the sheriff does, Jesus unbuckles his holster and lets the belt drop into the dust. He spreads his arms wide and starts walking toward us. We keep our hands on the hilts of our guns, too bewildered by his behavior to draw and start firing. When he reaches us, he takes the gun from our belt, empties the bullets, and pulls the bandana away from our faces. Then with his arms once again outstretched as on a cross, he beckons us to him. He calls to us to take one step toward him, one step down a new life-giving path, one step that will find us close enough for his arms to embrace us.

STEPPING INTO THE LIFE OF CHRIST

And in that embrace, our need to preserve those false selves starts fighting. We aren't ready to let go yet. We don't feel worthy of the love surrounding us. We can't imagine what life would look like. And so we try to fight. But our gun is in the dust. Our arms are pinned to our sides. The only thing left to us is to surrender those false selves into Jesus' care and to begin to let Jesus' life replace the half-lives we were leading. In the embrace, Jesus leans close and whispers, "If you want to come after me, say no to yourself, take up your cross, and follow me."

And so we deny the false selves that we have become, the small, scared people who stubbornly walked down the wrong paths. We lose the half-life we had when we stop trying to save it. And instead, we take on Christ's life. We step into the life of Christ as Paul says to the Galatians: "I have been crucified with Christ and I no longer live, but Christ lives in me. And the life that I now live in my body, I live by faith, indeed, by the faithfulness of God's Son, who loved me and gave himself for me" (Galatians 2:20).

Notice here that Paul says "by the faithfulness of God's Son." This could also be translated as *with faith in* God's Son." I like to think that this ambiguity is delightfully intentional. Both our faith in Jesus and Jesus' own utterly stalwart faithfulness give us the ability to live Christ's life. Jesus' faithfulness allows us the safety to cast off our false selves, and our faith propels us to take the leap and actually do away with them.

CHRIST IS ALIVE IN US

Truly, when we acknowledge Christ living in us, there is no room for the old life to hold sway. This life just ain't big enough for the both of them. But Christ's life is big enough to encompass and redeem the old life. The new paths we tread don't start out new, but as the old, life-taking paths we followed. We just travel them in the opposite direction. And as we journey back up those paths, Christ gives us the opportunity to repair and reconcile with those we've hurt and to reject and abandon the system that defines self with stuff. As Christ's life takes hold in us, we find that this new life is worth preserving, and not only preserving, but rejoicing in and sharing with others.

44

Isn't it wonderful that to change the life-taking path into the life-giving path is to surrender to Jesus and simply turn around? (This is the meaning of the word *repent,* by the way.)

Surrendering our outlaw lives and living Christ's life is not easy. That's why Jesus uses the imagery of the cross—not just because of his own impending execution, but because the cross is a symbol for suffering. Living Christ's life means sharing in the suffering of the world and also working to change the world to alleviate some of the suffering. But the good news is this: When we no longer live to preserve our false selves, but allow Christ to live in us, then we are never alone. We never have to face the joys and sorrows of this life alone. We never have to encounter suffering alone. The shoot-out ends without a shot fired. Our false selves are dead. And Christ is alive in us.

QUESTIONS

1. What does it mean to say no to ourselves? What is our cross (Mark 8:34)?

2. Why does Jesus discourage us in Mark 8:35 from saving our own lives? What does he mean by this?

3. What does it mean to be ashamed of Christ (Mark 8:38)? What are some examples of this? Why is Mark 8:38 so sobering?

4. How is a person made righteous (Galatians 2:16)? What is the connection between our faith and Christ's faithfulness?

5. How does dying to the law help us to live for God (Galatians 2:19)?

6. What does it mean to be crucified with Christ? How does one live by faith (Galatians 2:20)?

7. What does Galatians 2:21 tell us about the grace of God? Why is grace such an important part of understanding the Gospel?

8. What does Paul mean by being "found in" Christ (Philippians 3:9)?

9. What is righteousness? How does knowing Christ make us righteous (Philippians 3:10)?

10. Why does Paul speak of the resurrection of the dead as a goal to be reached (Philippians 3:11)?

11. How does someone know that he or she is going in the wrong direction? Why does Christ require us to change the direction we're going (to repent)?

4

THE PEACE OF JESUS
THE ABIDING PRESENCE OF GOD

SCRIPTURE
JOHN 20:19-29; PSALM 139:1-14

JOHN 20:19-29

[19]It was still the first day of the week. That evening, while the disciples were behind closed doors because they were afraid of the Jewish authorities, Jesus came and stood among them. He said, "Peace be with you." [20]After he said this, he showed them his hands and his side. When the disciples saw the Lord, they were filled with joy. [21]Jesus said to them again, "Peace be with you. As the Father sent me, so I am sending you." [22]Then he breathed on them and said, "Receive the Holy Spirit. [23]If you forgive anyone's sins, they are forgiven; if you don't forgive them, they aren't forgiven."

²⁴Thomas, the one called Didymus[a], one of the Twelve, wasn't with the disciples when Jesus came. ²⁵The other disciples told him, "We've seen the Lord!"

But he replied, "Unless I see the nail marks in his hands, put my finger in the wounds left by the nails, and put my hand into his side, I won't believe."

²⁶After eight days his disciples were again in a house and Thomas was with them. Even though the doors were locked, Jesus entered and stood among them. He said, "Peace be with you." ²⁷Then he said to Thomas, "Put your finger here. Look at my hands. Put your hand into my side. No more disbelief. Believe!"

²⁸Thomas responded to Jesus, "My Lord and my God!"

²⁹Jesus replied, "Do you believe because you see me? Happy are those who don't see and yet believe."

PSALM 139:1-14

¹LORD, you have examined me.
    You know me.
²You know when I sit down and when I stand up.
    Even from far away, you comprehend my plans.
³You study my traveling and resting.
    You are thoroughly familiar with all my ways.

---

a Or the twin

⁴There isn't a word on my tongue, Lord,

    that you don't already know completely.

⁵You surround me—front and back.

    You put your hand on me.

⁶That kind of knowledge is too much for me;

    it's so high above me that I can't fathom it.

⁷Where could I go to get away from your spirit?

    Where could I go to escape your presence?

⁸If I went up to heaven, you would be there.

    If I went down to the graveᵇ, you would be there too!

⁹If I could fly on the wings of dawn,

    stopping to rest only on the far side of the ocean—

      ¹⁰even there your hand would guide me;

      even there your strong hand would hold me tight!

¹¹If I said, "The darkness will definitely hide me;

    the light will become night around me,"

    ¹²even then the darkness isn't too dark for you!

    Nighttime would shine bright as day,

    because darkness is the same as light to you!

¹³You are the one who created my innermost parts;

    you knit me together while I was still in my mother's womb.

¹⁴I give thanks to you that I was marvelously set apart.

    Your works are wonderful—I know that very well.

---

b Hebrew *Sheol*

INSIGHT AND IDEAS

Some time ago, I received two rather large packages in the mail from my parents. Turns out they had been cleaning out closets in their house, and they decided for me that I would like to be in possession of all of the *Star Wars* memorabilia I collected when I was a kid. This includes about three-dozen action figures, none of which is old enough to really be worth anything and all of which are now taking up space in my closet, rather than in my parents'. Many of them are still in their boxes (yeah, I was *that* kid); and when I first got the packages in the mail, I spent an afternoon going through the boxes, trying to dredge up all of the intricate details I used to know about the *Star Wars* universe. I noticed that on the back of every action figure box an advertisement to purchase more action figures, which states: "The Force is with you in all the *Star Wars* figures and vehicles."

PEACE BE WITH YOU

Even if you don't know much about *Star Wars,* I'm sure you've heard the most famous line of dialogue from the films. And if you're an Episcopalian like I am, I'm also sure you that have a knee-jerk reaction to this line. Let's try: "May the Force be with you." (Did your mind immediately say, "And also with you.") I'd like to think that George Lucas borrowed and tweaked that bit of dialogue from the *Book of Common Prayer*. We say something similar three times during an average Sunday service at my church—at the beginning before the Collect ("The Lord be with you"), in the middle during the Peace ("The peace of the Lord be always with you"), and a few minutes later at the beginning of the Eucharistic Prayer ("The Lord be with you," again).

Let's focus on the middle one: "The peace of the Lord be always with you." (You thought, "And also with you," again, didn't you?) George Lucas might have borrowed his dialogue from us, but we borrowed ours from Jesus. Consider Jesus' words in the locked upper room on the day of his resurrection. (See John 20:19-23).

Twice in this short passage (and once more a few verses and a week later), the Risen Christ says to his disciples: "Peace be with you." (They aren't Episcopalians; so they aren't trained to say, "And also with you," back to him.) On one level, Jesus' saying, "Peace be with you," is just a greeting to the disciples. And he has to repeat this greeting after showing them his maimed hands and side because they don't recognize him the first time around. But as the words of the Gospel according to John so often do, even something as simple as a greeting is loaded with layers of meaning.

So what is this "peace" that Jesus offers to the disciples when he appears to them on the evening of the first day of the week, the day he rose from the dead? There are at least four layers of peace here in this passage. There are certainly more layers, but we'll focus on four. Going deeper into Jesus' peace as we reflect on this passage of Scripture helps us find that peace more readily in our own lives.

LAYERS OF PEACE

The surface level is the greeting still heard today in Hebrew and Arabic speaking countries. *Shalom* and *Salaam*—one wonders how there can be so much conflict between and among peoples in these countries—countries such as Syria, Israel, Iran—when their special words for greeting one another mean "peace." How wonderful would this world be— how much closer to the kingdom we pray is coming—were we to always greet one another with "peace" and mean it?

On the level below the surface, Jesus' word of peace to the disciples acknowledges their current situation. There they are, huddled together in the house—shutters drawn, candles snuffed, door locked for fear of the people who colluded to put Jesus to death. Would the disciples be next? Would the chief priests and the council be satisfied with the blood of the leader, or would they pursue the followers too? How had the disciples gotten everything so wrong? How could they have followed someone so disposable, so utterly breakable as Jesus turned out to be?

PEACE REPLACES FEAR

And into their fear, their confusion, their uncertainty the Risen Christ comes and says, "Peace be with you." He comes to them even though the door is barricaded. He comes to them even though three days earlier he had died an excruciating death on the cross. He comes to them even though they aren't expecting him, even though they haven't understood what he'd told them about who he is.

And when Jesus gives them peace, their fear turns into joy. Fear, confusion, and uncertainty have a tendency to hollow us out, to make us feel empty. But peace has a way of filling up all the cracks and corners. As Paul says to the church in Rome: "May the God of hope fill you with all joy and peace in faith so that you overflow with hope by the power of the Holy Spirit" (Romans 15:13). Peace fills us up. When Jesus gives his peace to us, we notice it leaving no place for fear to gain a foothold within.

But let's not stop there; let's go a level deeper. When the Risen Christ offers the disciples peace, he is offering them more than a greeting and an antidote for fear. He is offering them "the abiding presence of God." This is how a member of my church's Wednesday Bible study group described what "peace" means to her, and I adore this definition. Peace is not simply the absence of conflict. Peace is "the abiding presence of God." Peace happens when we attune ourselves to God's abiding presence. Peace happens when we resonate with God's movement in our lives. Peace happens when we discover the inner serenity that God provides in the midst of the maelstrom of activity that marks our lives today.

CHRIST IS ALWAYS WITH US

This truth might naturally drive us to conclude that the peace, which the Risen Christ offers to the disciples and to us, would excuse us from the pain and suffering that life sometimes brings. But Jesus never promised us a reprieve from tragedy. Rather, he promised something so much greater: He promised to be with us always to the end of the ages (remember our first session about Jesus' name). He promised to suffer with us, to cry with us, to break his heart open when our hearts break and pour his heart's love on our wounds. There is no door we can pass through that the abiding presence of God has not already entered. There is no depth or height that we can attain and not be where God already is. As the psalmist says in one of the most beautiful passages in the Book of Psalms:

> Where could I go to get away from your spirit?
>   Where could I go to escape your presence?
> If I went up to heaven, you would be there.
>   If I went down to the grave[c], you would be there too!
> (Psalm 139:7-8)

But all too often we forget that God's presence abides, and we fail to look for God in situations where we conclude that God couldn't possibly be. And yet how many of us have said at one time or another, "I just need a moment's peace." By our definition, when we say that, what we are really saying is, "I just need a moment to remind myself that I am in God's abiding presence, a moment to drink in God's love, a moment to be folded into the arms of grace." These are the ingredients for the "peace" Jesus offers us.

PEACE COMES WITH A MISSION

And yet there is another level deeper still. When the Risen Christ offers peace to the disciples, the peace comes with

---

c Hebrew *Sheol*

a mission: "Peace be with you," says Jesus. "As the Father sent me, so I am sending you" (John 20:21). And then he breathes on them, saying, "Receive the Holy Spirit." Thus, Jesus not only gives them the word of peace, he also breathes God's abiding presence into them through the power of the Holy Spirit. The Father has sent Jesus to bring peace, and now Jesus commissions the disciples and us to do the same. The peace that Jesus offers is not for us alone, but for us to share with this damaged, broken world.

Paul offers this mission to the church in Philippi, and he girds it with the strength of God's peace:

> Be glad in the Lord always! Again I say, be glad! Let your gentleness show in your treatment of all people. The Lord is near. Don't be anxious about anything; rather, bring up all of your requests to God in your prayers and petitions, along with giving thanks. Then the peace of God that exceeds all understanding will keep your hearts and minds safe in Christ Jesus.
>
> From now on, brothers and sisters, if anything is excellent and if anything is admirable, focus your thoughts on these things: all that is true, all that is holy, all that is just, all that is pure, all that is lovely, and all that is worthy of praise. Practice these things: whatever you learned, received, heard, or saw in us. The God of peace will be with you. (Philippians 4:4-9)

Remember the first level of peace: the simple greeting of the Arabic speaking world. We can make this our greeting as well—and not just our greeting but our mission. Just think how powerful an act it is to greet someone with God's peace. In the simple words "Peace be with you," we bring with us greetings from our Lord. We bring with us the joy that quells fear and uncertainty. And we bring with us the abiding presence of God and of the Risen Christ. Now just imagine: If we were to take this greeting we practice in church and carry the peace of the Lord into every handshake, every wave, every high-five, every tilt of the head, every smile of recognition, every embrace, then we would change the world.

QUESTIONS

1. Why, do you suppose, does Jesus say, "Peace be with you," in this post-resurrection encounter with his disciples (John 20:19)? Why does he then show them his hands and his side (John 20:20)?

2. What is the significance of the disciples' being filled with joy (John 20:20)?

3. What might the disciples have been feeling when Jesus told them, "As the Father sent me, so I am sending you"(John 20:21)?

4. How does Christ's imparting of the Holy Spirit in John 20:22 relate to the coming of the Holy Spirit fifty days later in Acts 2?

5. What does Jesus mean in John 20:23? How does this apply to us today?

6. Compared with the other disciples (who have already seen Jesus' hands and side), is Thomas at a significant faith disadvantage (John 20:25)?

7. Why does Jesus say that people who believe without seeing are happy (John 20:29)? What about those who believe only after they see?

8. Psalm 139 describes God's omnipresence. How does this concept bring us peace? Is God's presence the same everywhere?

9. In what ways are we empowered to carry the peace of Jesus into the world?

CONVERGE

Bible Studies

WOMEN OF THE BIBLE
by James A. Harnish
9781426771545

OUR COMMON SINS
by Dottie Escobedo-Frank
9781426768989

WHO YOU ARE IN CHRIST
by Shane Raynor
9781426771538

SHARING THE GOSPEL
by Curtis Zackery
9781426771569

KINGDOM BUILDING
by Grace Biskie
9781426771576

And more to come.

PRACTICAL PRAYER
by Joseph Yoo
9781426778254

RECLAIMING ANGER
by David Dorn
9781426771552

THREE GIFTS, ONE CHRIST
by Katie Z. Dawson
9781426778278

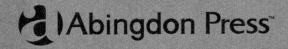

Abingdon Press

BKM136600011 PACP01383978-01

CPSIA information can be obtained
at www.ICGtesting.com
Printed in the USA
BVOW08s2158231216
471780BV00005B/13/P